BE HERE NOW
EVERYWHERE

Gurudev Sri Sri Ravi Shankar

RIGI PUBLICATION

BE HERE NOW EVERYWHERE
GURUDEV SRI SRI RAVI SHANKAR

BY

Dr. K.V. Indulekha MSc.Ph.D

Originally published in India

ISBN: 978-93-88393-45-4 (Paperback)
ISBN: 978-93-88393-46-1   (eBook)

Published by RIGI PUBLICATION

777, Street no.9, Krishna Nagar
Khanna-141401 (Punjab), India
Website: www.rigipublication.com
Email: info@rigipublication.com
Phone: +91-9357710014, +91-9465468291

UNIVERSAL PRAYER

I prostrate to the Universal Teacher

Who is absolute truth

Pure consciousness and Bliss

Who is beyond all differences

Who is even full

without attributes –

Formless

Who is all pervading and

ever centered in the self.

<u>PREFACE</u>

Gurudev Sri Sri Ravi Sankar is as deep as and as vast as an ocean in all perspectives specially in the case of wisdom and knowledge. Listening and reading the matters put forward by his Holiness make me feel that I am in a Wonder Land - Many a times I wonder, who is that a person could be such a store house of knowledge ? How could everything be at the finger tips of a person, ancient and as well as modern thoughts ?

In such an amazement a thought started developing in me why shouldn't I collect some information which would be useful for everyday life of each person. If I could bring out such dearth of an information it would really benefit the ordinary people. At present this wisdom is scattered here and there in audio-video, Cds, books, social media etc. etc.

Though my attempt would reach only to a meagre level I decided to move forward. I could humbly bring out in a co-ordinated way few information which an ordinary person can grasp and put it in practice. The Knowledge of the Master included here is in the same way as presented by him.

Surrendering at the louts feet of Gurudev I put forward the Pearls of Wisdom to all the people who come in contact with it.

Jai Gurudev

Dr. K.V Indulekha.

drkvindulekha@yahoo.com

I PROMISE

If I had to promise you something what would it be?
I can't promise that you would always be comfortable
Because comfort brings boredom and discomfort
I can't promise that all your desires will be fulfilled
Because desires whether fulfilled or unfulfilled bring frustration
I can't promise that there will always be good times
Because it is the toughest times that makes us appreciate joy
I can't promise that we will be rich or famous or powerful
Because they can all be pathways to misery
I can't promise that we will always be together
Because it is separation that make togetherness so wonderful,
Yet if you are willing to walk with me,
If you are willing to value love over everything else
Promise that this will be this most rich and fulfilling life possible.
I promise your life will be an eternal celebration.
I promise that I will cherish you
More than a king cherishes his crown
And I shall love you more than a mother loves her new born
If you are willing to walk into my arms
If you are willing to live in my heart,
You will find the one you have waited forever
You will meet yourself in my arms
I promise

Gurudev H.H Sri Sri Ravi Shankar
(Gurudev Sri. Sri.)

WHAT IS BOTHERING YOU

Tell me what is bothering you? A prayer which is not answered on time or you feel I don't listen to you? I listen to each and every prayer you put in front of me. I watch everything you do and I know what you are going through and what is going on in your mind. I am worried for you.

Some blessings are delayed but never go unanswered/ I only give you what you need at this point of time not what you want. You have to trust me, you must remain calm in adverse situations, call on your faith that you have on me. Don't rush to the conclusions that I don't hear what you say. I am sitting right here to cleanse your karmas. Let me do my work because I only know what is right for you and get from God Almighty. Till then hold me tightly. Talk to me, share every single thing with me as you share with your friends and family. They are there till the time you have this life. They can support you, but I am the one who brought you here and will take you to the end. My love for you is infinite and endless. Just wait patiently for the bad time to get over.

Gurudev Sri. Sri.

GURU

See this word called "Guru" has been wrongly understood. The moment you say Guru, then it is no more a man, woman or a human.

When you are surrendering to the Guru, you are not surrendering to the outer structure but you are seeing light behind this body, the love behind the body, the space inside the body. If you cannot surrender to the Guru, you cannot surrender to anybody else. It is impossible because everybody else will appear to be more frightening.

Master on his own will never give any suggestion to anybody, anytime. But when asked for he will give you something and if you follow that, that will be the best for you. If you don't follow it, you will go through a circuitous route. You will have some problems and cry for a few days. But then Master is never angry that you didn't listen. It is okay - learn the hard way. Go through something. So what? Still Master says, "I am here by your side." He says, "You can avoid unwanted sufferings, but if you want to go through it, well go ahead. You will grow through that also." Guru doesn't care whether the person feels good or does not feel good. Just do what is good for the person.

The consciousness is so abstract. It is very difficult to perceive it without something you consider concrete. A Guru is like a window where you have this hope that if this mind can get to the highest, I can also get there. The window is there. When you stand near the window, you can see the infinite sky.

The same thing with a Master. He is like a window. The sky is everywhere. It is also behind the wall and above the ceiling, but it is not visible. You can only see the sky if you can come near the window. The window is hollow and empty. It is so transparent that through it, you can glimpse that just this is not the end. What I see as a wall, or as an ending, is not the end; but through this window I can see that there is infinity. There is something beyond. That glimpse of infinity comes. That is the purpose. You get a glimpse of how much God or nature loves you through the love of the Master.

But in Guru, at least there is no self interest of any kind at all. He is totally hollow and empty; there are no vasanas, or desires, in his mind. There is nothing that a Guru wants from you or will force you to do. Guru does not want a thing from you other than your own joy. Guru's love is unconditional and spontaneous.

A Guru is not one who claims authority on you or dictates terms to you. A Guru simply means one who brings more joy, alertness and awareness into your life. He is the one who helps you get in touch with yourself, who reminds you to live in the present moment, who pulls you out of your guilt, agitation, sorrow, anguish and allows you to be yourself. Also, a Master lives the values he teaches.

Gurudev Sri. Sri.

His Holiness
Sri Sri Ravi Shankar
(Gurudev Sri. Sri.)

His Holiness Sri Sri Ravi Shankar is a Universally revered spiritual and humanitarian leader. His vision of a violence-free, stress-free society through the reawakening of human values has inspired millions to broaden their spheres of responsibility and work towards the betterment of the world. Born in 1956 in southern India, Sri Sri was often found deep in meditation as a child. At the age of four, he astonished his teachers by reciting the Bhagavad Gita, an ancient Sanskrit scripture. He has always had the unique gift of presenting the deepest truths in the simplest of words.

Sri Sri established the Art of Living, an educational and humanitarian Non-Governmental Organisation that works in special consultative status with the Economic and Social Council (ECOSOC) of the United Nations in 1981. Present in over 155 countries, it formulates and implements lasting solutions to conflicts and issues faced by individuals, communities and nations. In 1997, he founded the International Association for Human Values (IAHV) to foster human values and lead sustainable development projects. Sri Sri has reached out to more than 300 million people worldwide through personal interactions, public events, teachings, Art of Living workshops and humanitarian initiatives. He has brought to the masses ancient practices which were traditionally kept exclusive, and has designed many self development techniques which can easily be integrated into daily life to calm the mind and instill confidence and enthusiasm. One of Sri Sri's most unique offerings to the world is the Sudarshan Kriya, a powerful breathing technique that facilitates physical, mental, emotional and social well-being.

Numerous honours have been bestowed upon Sri Sri, including National and International.

Contents

GURU BRAHMA
GURU VISHNU
GURU DEVO
MAHESHWARAH
GURU SAAKSHAAT
PARA BRAHMA
TASMAI SHRI
GURUVEH NAMAHA
TASMAI SHRI
GURUVEH NAMAHA

PART - 1
MIND EMOTIONS AND THOUGHTS

PART I

MIND EMOTIONS AND THOUGHTS

BIG MIND

You know there is a big mind and a small mind. Sometimes the big mind wins over the small mind and sometimes it is the other way around.

When the small mind wins over, it is misery and when the big mind wins, it is joy.

Small mind promises joy and leaves your hand empty. Big mind may bring resistance in the beginning but fills you with joy.

The word Guru means great. Jay means victory. Deva means one who is fun-loving, playful, light. One who is playful is often not dignified and when one is dignified, he is often not playful.

"Jai Guru Dev" is victory to the big mind in you that is both dignified and playful. That is what Jai Guru Dev means: "Victory to the Greatness in you."

You do not say victory or hail to the Master as he has won already. You say victory to your own Self, your own mind, which is being veiled by the small mind.

(Gurudev Sri. Sri.)

MYSTERY OF THE MIND

The mind is the biggest mystery Your own mind can be your best friend and you worst enemy. The mind is responsible for our happiness as well as our misery. When the mind is in the present moment, every thing appears to be beautiful. However when the mind is in a mess even in the best of places it can find a thousand reasons to be miserable.

There are five modulations of the mind.

1. The mind wants proof for everything. How can you get proof for every thing? Impossible.

2. The mind does not understand things the way they actually are. But thinks something else. You thought something, a little later found out that it was not actually that way. A little later concepts break down. This is called Viparyaya

3. The third, the mind has its own imagination, when nothing of that sort actually exists.

4. The mind falls asleep, if it is not thinking of anything then it falls asleep.

5. The mind is stuck in the memory of the past or worried about the future.

These five modulations prevent one from being alive in the present moment and enjoying it.

Yoga brings the shift, it helps you to sail over modulations of the mind. How is this possible? First is to know that you are going to have everything here and go. You are not going to take anything with you when you leave the world. The cause of miseries is holding on to things, mine mine, mine.

(Gurudev Sri. Sri.)

TWO TYPES OF OBSTACLES

Whenever you do any work, in that there are two types of obstacles. One is associated with mind (Buddhi) and other is perfection (Siddhi) ability to do any work flawlessly. If you want to do any work perfectly there are challenges or obstacles. Isn't it? In the same manner mind also creates obstacles.

If good thoughts come to mind then work is done. But if there is negativity in thought then work will just get stuck. So in order to do any work there has to be mind (buddhi) or thought behind it to do that work. Along with what we need is effectiveness. For example if the operation was successful but the patient died it is no use, isn't it? It means Siddhi is not there.

What is Siddhi? It is the ability to get the work done in the same manner as it was to be completed. To get any work done without any flaw is Siddhi. There is a saying in Kannada which means when there were teeth that time peanut were not there and when peanuts were there no teeth left. You got the peanut but this will not be called as Siddhi. That which you get well in advance from needed time and in more quantity than it was supposed to be then that is Siddhi. And even to receive before time or on time and with right quantity is also Siddhi. And to remove both types of obstacles needs Grace of God. Mind should be sharp, sathivik (positive) and Siddhi should be on time. Siddhi mean contentment. Let it happen what it has to happen. That which fulfills desire even before it arises. This is Siddhi.

And Buddhi is that mind which ensures that there are no desires and even if there are then the mind should watch when this desire arises and know that desire is nothing. This is completeness. So you all pray that let your mind be positive and also at siddhi for the work. Whatever you do should be successful.

(Gurudev Sri. Sri.)

ROLE OF PAIN IN PERSONAL & SPIRITUAL TRANSFORMATION

Que: Gurudev what is role of pain in personal and spiritual transformation?

Gurudev : Pain is inevitable, suffering is optional. You have heard that before, right? Pain is nothing but intense sensation. Yet, do not justify or encourage pain. Some people tend to justify and encourage pain and this is where masochism starts. You need to stay clear masochism and that is why I would say if pain comes it has come due to some Karma that is, it moves on.

The principle of Karma is such a healthy thing to save the mind, it is such good vaccination for mind. When you say Karma then you are able let go and move on. Otherwise you brood over what ever has happened in the past and you try to limit the thing with some cause. If you look back whatever you thought as cause is also an effect, it is not the cause. Every time you fix something as the cause of an effect, you have erred. You have seen that it is true and has not stood the test of time. No cause has stood the test of time because very cause is an effect. This is the spiritual way. Even you think in this direction and go deeper to the ultimate cause, you find that the only one thing that is the cause of the entire existence. With the one realisation your peace can never been taken away by anybody or any incident on the planet nothing can move you if you know the cause.

That is why there is beautiful verse in Sanskrit 'Tasmain nama parama, karana, karanaya'. Shiva you are the cause of all causes. The grand time that is beyond time, otherwise we keep going round in the cycle of karma. As it can be little confusing if you don't pay very keen attention to what I am saying. One is karma that is cause and effect. Another is going beyond karma- how do you get out of the cycle karma. Are you getting this, you have to ponder on this once more. This principle of karma is big blessing for you to let go and move further.

(Gurudev Sri. Sri.)

MIND, TIME & PLANETS
The Connection Between Mind Time and Planets

Do you know, when the time changes the mind also changes. There is a beautiful sense about this. You can also get a clue from an astrological chart, how the mind is connected with time.

There are 12 constellation and 9 planets according to Vedic astrology. It is said that when Jupitar transits in the 8th place from the time you are born it has an impact on your mind. Similarly when Saturn transits the 8th place, it makes your emotion go topsy turvy. When Jupiter is in the 8th place you lose all your wisdom. but that is only 11 months that it make you so miserable. Unless and until you are in deep spiritual knowledge and enlightened this will definitely affect your mind.

Similarly every two and half days the mood of the mind changes. If you are miserable it won't exceed two and half days. There will be a break and then it may come again since the cosmos has an influence on the mind.

Know that all this positive emotions are just passing phase. It may be because of some planetary combination. This is where astrology comes to you to help in a big way. That is why Jyotish (Astrology) is called Eye of wisdom. It means you see beyond your immediate situation and know that its only for some time, and it is going to change. From this you gain some unknown inner strength and you will not start planning for yourself or people around you. It is always better to blame planets because you are so far away, you can't do any thing about them. they move at their own pace. You can't hasten their movements. On top of the planets is Lord Shiva or Shiva Tattva. So by chanting 'Om Nama Shivaya'. you will sail through all this.

I tell you, in any of these unfavorable situation there is always an advantage, that is moving inward and becoming more spiritual. In favorable situations your mind is outward so that at large in unfavorable situation you can turn mind inward and utilize this time for prayers and meditation.

If you are already inward you do not have anything to do. So there will not be any problem also. Even if problems are there it would be minimum, they will just come and go. So every situation can be used for one's benefit.

(Gurudev Sri. Sri.)

LOVE, FEAR, HATRED, AND SURRENDER
The Secret Of Love, Fear, Hatred And Surrender

Surrender means an unshakable confidence. Surrender simply means un conditional love. When there is love there is no fear. This is one energy that functioned in three forms either love, fear or hatred. When there is hatred there is no fear. When there is fear there is no love or hate. And with all these three some actions in the body is at particular place, the heart, whether you are in fear, deep love or in hatred

And they are inter changeable. One changes into the other. You love somebody and this love slowly change into hatred or as your love some, they move dearly and the fear arises thinking Oh! I may lose it. What ever you love must you hold on to so the same love has changed itself to fear.

So when surrender happens you cannot do anything about it. If you love something very deep then surrender. Surrender is not a power, not a fear, not something which comes out of force. It is a spontaneous happening. Only the strong can surrender, the weak can never surrender. But we seem to understand it in the other way. We feel that someone if weak they will surrender. I am powerful how can I surrender? No, to surrender it takes great courage and power, strength and confidence, only then you can surrender.

Surrender is always unconditional. It is not that ' I surrender, so I can have peace of mind and blessing or whatever. It is not surrender, you love someone because what they are, then you don't love them. You love the quality.

Love is very deep intimate phenomenon in your consciousness. It just flowers. It cannot but flower. There is no way you can meddle forth it. You go near love , you dissolve, you simply don't exist. That is the definition of love. Either you remain in love or remain as somebody. Either you are there or here is love. You can never meet love or you can never love.

See in conversation we say ' see I love that because....' it is the most stupid thing. You love something and say I love you because you are good person. You love those qualities. And there is nothing great in you loving these qualities. And I tell you seem to love these qualities which you don't have. That is how people make ideals and they remain far away from ideals.

When we remain as small pond, a stone will create a big ripple. When somebody says something that can blow your peace off. So this peace is thrown off by people around you. When you become an ocean even a big mountain falling into it does not affect it. That is the wonder.

(Gurudev Sri. Sri.)

ATTITUDES TO HANDLE THE MIND

Four kinds of attitudes you Can develop to handle your own mind

1. Friendliness – Be friendly with people who are happy. If your are not friendly with happy people you will be jealous. This is because you think that your enemy is happy and you cannot feel so. Your enemy being happy, so should have friends with happy people. Such an attitude does a lot of good into your mind.

2. Compassion – Do not be friendly with the people who are miserable. Instead have compassion for them, if you are friendly you will be unhappy. You can never help them to come out of their misery.

   Many people have gotten into trouble by being friendly with unhappy people, both become miserable. It is like a doctor going to a patient who is sick and doctor also become sick. If the doctor also think ' How can I alone be healthy? let me also share the patient's misery. Who will help the patient then? So what should be the attitude with the people who are miserable? compassion, not pity.

3. Happiness – For people who are doing good work or who is successful in the world you should feel happy as though you are doing it. For example some one is good singer singing and bringing joy to everybody, seeing him you should think, I feel so happy that this person is singing so well and making one happy. If someone is good entertainer and he entertain everybody feel everyone happy about it, if someone is great architect and builds beautiful building you should feel happy about it. Whenever someone is doing a good job share that happiness with them. We need to have this attitude.

4. Indifference – For people who, doing horrible things in the society destroying themselves we usually get angry at them. When you are angry your mind suffers a huge loss. You lose so much energy, you lose your mood and enthusiasm goes away from you. You become angry and

you are no better than the other person. You do not know what you are doing. So what should you do in such a situation? Have sort of indifference in your mind. For example there are thieves in the world. They are there, what can you do about them? First accept, and be indifferent. However this does not mean you do not take any action. Your mind is indifferent (unaffected) but you act out.

These are four attitudes that will help us to save our mind. That is what we need to do. Save our mind at all costs.

(Gurudev Sri. Sri.)

FACTORS INFLUENCING THE MIND
Five factors that influence the mind

Place, Time, Food, Past Impression, and Association and Actions. Every place you are in has different impact on the mind. Even in your home you can see that you feel different in different rooms. A place where has been singing, chanting and meditation has different influence on the mind. Suppose you like a particular place your mind finds that a little later it will not be same.

Time is also a factor. Different times of the day and year have different influence on the mind. Different types of food that you take influence you for the same day.

The past impressions, the karma have a different impact on you mind. Awareness about knowledge and meditation all help erase the past impressions.

Association and actions. The people events that you are associated with do influence your mind and your actions and association effect your mind. In certain company your mind behave in one way and with the other in different way.

(Gurudev Sri. Sri.)

YOU CANNOT MAKE ANYBODY HAPPY

In this world there is always a play of positive and negative. Some problems come some challenges come and solutions also follow. The ancient people would simply focus on keeping their energy high. If your energy is high and people come to you their problems will get solved. What happen when people talk to you about their problems. You get steeped in their problems. You get carried away with the problem. So try this. Let everybody come and complain hundred things to you. You simply keep your energy, high. Your see inward your mind inwards as though nothing has happened. You will realise that there is freedom within you.

Try this – anybody can complain on anything and let the world go topsy truvey- But hold on to the idea – I am going to keep my energy, you just take one such steps and then see. 'Problems and challenges come so that you can turn your mind inwards.

Instead of turning the mind inwards when problems come what one do? We chase the problem and get completely drawn in that direction, and then our energy goes down and we collapse. Many a times in the name of compassion and sympathy you get drowned. Your compassion does not really help at all in solving problem.

It may sound very severe but in compassion the problem multiplies and doesn't get solved. Problems can also make a person turn inwards and look inside, get in a state of dispassion and calmness, instead you give reasons and try to pacify the person.

Pacifying a person is the worst thing. You should not pacify them. Let everybody carry their own cross, bear their karma. If you are miserable or happy, it is your karma. So you choose your karma.

This attitude makes a person more independent. You show compassion and they seek more attention. You feel more and more compassionate and give them more attention and then neither the compassion nor attention is possible. It breeds tension in you. That poor person is so unpleasant and I have to make him happy. To make someone happy is a big burden. Don't try to do that at all. This is a new policy don't try to make anybody happy, you can't. There is Sanskrit proverb 'Kashtasya Sukasya Napoidata' nobody gives happiness or misery. It is created by ones own self – one's own mind.

(Gurudev Sri. Sri.)

GENTLE MAN AND SNAKE

What lesson did the gentleman learn from the snake?

It was a dark night a gentleman was going into a forest, with his small torch. From a distance he saw a snake on the path. He stood there waiting to snake to move. His torch cells (battery) were running out. There was a very feeble light. If it was totally dark he would have passed. But it wasn't – there was a feeble light- so could see the snake. He was frightened. He stood there sweating and shivering. And snake was seen to be very adamant. It never moved. It seemed to say that it will move if he moved. That it will not move since he did not move. It was very frightening for him. He waited and waited for three to four hours. By that time another person came along with the more powerful torch. He checked and discovered it was not snake but just a rope. There was big sigh of relief. He wondered at his foolishness that he had wasted so much time, shivering and getting angry fearing this snake moving and it was just rope.

Something which appeared to the big burden, problem which would seem to take away life later became a joke. The gentleman laughed and laughed the rest of the way. Then the day broke and the entire forest was filled with flowers fruits and celebrations. Birds were singing peacocks were dancing and the streams were flowing. That place which was frightening in the dark night now became a place of celebration.

This very universe and very events in the world which appear to us to be a big botheration turns around and become a playing field, a game. When you can see the whole plan of events as temporary as non existing, then even when someone could sometime notice the button being pushed that 'something is happening'. Oh! what is happening here inside? I am getting angry, I am feeling frustrated Oh! God. Every event, every happening become a play, a game, a celebration. Walk blissfully, breath blissfully, see blissfully, being aware of all these events.

When you see the entire events as fleeting imposition or happening and you remain untouched by them you are happy, joy springs out of you as a big fountain. That is your very nature.

(Gurudev Sri. Sri.)

CLEARING OF NEGATIVE THOUGHTS
Seven ways to clear your Negative Thoughts

1. **Get busy**
    When you recognise a negative thought get busy If you simply sit, you will keep thinking a lot.

2. **Improve circulation in your body**
    If your head is filled with too many thought, lie down on the floor and keep rolling and you will see the circulation in the body improves, then the mind feels better. That is the reason they do Shayana Pradakhinam (a form of worship done by rolling on the floor). Experience it and see how there is a change in your mind.

3. **Shake hands with negative thoughts**

If you keep resisting negative thoughts and try to push them away, then they will follow you like a ghost. Shake hands with your negative thoughts, tell them come here and sit with me I will not leave you!' and you will see how quickly they disappear. Thoughts are scared of it. If you get scared of negative thoughts then they will control you. But if you shake hands with them they will disappear.

4. **Pranayama and meditation.**
   Pranayam and meditations are the best way to apply brakes in buzzing mind. It is very effective and instantly calm your mind down.

5. **Intestinal cleansing**
   If you are bombarded with too many negative thoughts, know that something must be wrong with your bowel movement. Do Shank Prakshalan (intestinal cleansing), that will also help.

6. **Improve circulation**
   Get up, do some exercise, sing, dance, do yoga, meditation, pranayama, all these will help you.

7. **Become a witness to your thoughts**
   We cannot stop a thoughts or know a thought before it comes.

And when it comes, it also goes away immediately. If you are witness to the thoughts it simply drifts away and vanishes.

But if you hold to it and chew it, then it stays with you.

Thoughts come and go and that which is the basis of thoughts is the Atma (Soul) and that is what you are. You are like the sky and the thoughts are like clouds. This could be the nearest example one can give. Clouds come and go in the sky, But can they disturb or limit, the vastness of the sky in any way?

No, not at all

So when you fly above the clouds, when you go beyond the clouds you see that the sky is untouched. It is the same. It is unchanged. It is only the thoughts which keep moving. That is what happen in meditation.

When you come into 'Sakshi Bhav' that is when you simply become a witness to the thoughts we do not have to attach ourselves to the thoughts. That is foolishness. Whether they are good thoughts or bad thoughts they come and go. You are far above and beyond all this. This is called 'Vihangam marg'. It means rising above thoughts and seeing that you have nothing to do with these moving thoughts.

(Gurudev Sri. Sri.)

LOVE AND LUST - OVER COMING LUST

What is the difference between love and lust How to overcome lust

1.	Love brings relaxation :	Lust brings tension
2.	Love causes longing and pain	Lust causes fervourishness and frustration
3.	Love bring sacrifice	Lust:brings violence
4.	In love you want to give and surrender	In lust you want to grab and posses
5.	Love says I want and have what you want	All I want you to have is what I want.
6.	Love is effortless	In lust there is effort
7.	Love liberates and sets you free	Lust imprisons and destroys
8.	Love commands	Lust:demands

How to overcome lust

First of all don't make a big deal out of it. To get over it, there are four things that really help a lot.

1. Do some creative stuff – lust, will simply not bother you when you have hobby.

2. Physical Exercise – go jogging, swimming, to the gym,

do Suryanamaskar.

Sweat it out. It is good for your body and mind and definitely great to get over any obsession.

3. Dancing- Dance to some devotional music, even some soft, pop or rock.

Move your body with eyes closed, surrender to the music.

4. And finally cold water shower.

(Gurudev Sri. Sri.)

PRANA - LIFE FORCE ENERGY, MEDITATIONS AND YOGA

PRANA – LIFE FORCE ENERGY, MEDITATION AND YOGA

MEDITATION

Meditation is food for soul, it nurtures the core of your existence. Meditation has multiple benefits, it keeps you physically fit and healthy mentally fcused and sane. Intellectually it brings such sharpness keenness of attention awareness and observation.

Emotionally you feel lighter, softer and purer. You are able to let go of all the past garbage. It creates positive vibrations around you, influences your behaviour with other and behaviour with you. Meditation gives the deepest rest in the shortest time.

Meditation will help to develop the following charcteristics

Santi	:	Peace
Dama	:	Control over five senses
Thridishta	:	Equanimity
Uparathi	:	Do action with total involements
Shradha	:	Centeredness

Samadhan	:	Satisfaction
Vairagya	:	No craving – contentment
Viveka	:	Discrimination
Curiosity	:	about nature and actions

(Gurudev Sri. Sri.)

PRANA OR LIFE FORCE ENERGY
What is Prana or life force energy?

There is a lot to know about Prana. The breath is connected to neuro physiology. When the left nostril is dominating the right side of the brain is active. When the right nostril is functioning, the left side of the brain (logic, thinking and understanding) is active. When breath predominantly go in and out through right nostril and very little through the left nostril you listen and enjoy without understanding the knowledge like it is music. When the breath flows equally through both nostrils meditation and prayer happen or nothing happens.

If you are in the presence of someone who is very spiritual then both nostrils will flow equally. If you come to meet a Guru or pass by a temple church on a place of worship or spiritual activity, you will find both nostrils equally functioning. Prana or life force moves through the neuron through the nostrils. There are three nadis. (1) Sun nadi is the right nostril (2) the Moon nadi is the left nostril (3) the fire nadi is in between both. This is known as Sushumna nadi. We are living in the ocean of prana. Prana and truth or consciousness is the prana of prana.

The five types of prana in the body are Prana Apana, Udana, Samana,Vyana.

Prana is the energy in the upper part of the body, in the region above heart. If prana is high or imbalanced you cannot sleep. Apana Vayu is the energy in the lower part of the body. If the prana is too high you feel lethargic, sleepy. Samana vayu is in the stomach region and it aids in digestion.

Udana Vayu is in the upper chest and throat region. It is responsible for emotions. If Udna vayu is imbalanced you have no emotion. You become like a stone or you become so messy and weak.

Vyana is all over the body. It is responsible for movements in the joints, the circulation in the body. If Vyana prana is disturbed your joints are not flexible. There are aches and pains. Punch prana the different types of prana are present in every body and different pranas dominates at different times. The imbalances in the prana are corrected during Pranayama and Sudarshan kriya.

To understand prana takes along time. There are 1,72,000 nadis or prana channels which function in our body.

The breath changes with every action and certain prana function at certain times. The Vedas teach us that this metabolism of your body is twice when you are breathing through the right nostrils than it is when breathing through the left. Following this when the left nostril functions it is good time to drink. When right is functioning then it is good time to eat. If you do the reverse then within in six months you may fall sick.

Ayurveda also says that you should not eat and drink at the same time. And when you do so you should give a gap of half an hour to one hour before drinking. The breath changes every hour. similarly prana changes energy in the world, changing all the time.

(Gurudev Sri. Sri.)

SUDARSHAN KRIYA AND CURING ILLNESS

Que: How does Sudarshan kriya help in curing illnesses?

Gurudev: you know that Sudarshan kriya helps in preventing many ilnesses – A professor who is working on genes in Oslo University Norway says that there are 300 chromosomes which are responsible for hypertension, cancer etc. And Pranayama and Sudharshan kriya suppresses these 300 chromosomes. So if one keep practicing these techniques there are less and less chance for getting these illnesses.

MEDITATION MERGING INTO SELF

Que: Gurudev when I am meditating is it the mind that is meditating or who is meditating.

Gurudev: When you are meditating it is the mind merging into the self, that is what meditation. The wave is getting back to the ocean. Now you cannot ask me who is getting back, is the wave getting into the ocean or ocean getting into the wave. So merging of the wave and ocean is meditation, mind and being is the meditation.

YOGA AND KUNDALINI YOGA

Que: I am very interested in Yoga. I have started training on the Kundalini yoga.
Can you talk about importance of Yoga and about Kundalini yoga?

Gurudev: I would recommend you not to go into Kundalini yoga and all these things. It is any way coming up naturally. You have done the Sudharshan kriya, Sakti kriya and Advance Meditaion course and it is moving very smoothly and very well.

I have seen many people forcibly moving the Kundlini and they lose balance in life. They lose their sleep and they get the problems.. I have seen many people to have literally go crazy because there are some types of Yoga which are not suitable for today's age. In ancient days they have lot of time - 12 years they would stay and slowly they would do these practices. They have nothing much to do. But today they give you the Kundalini yoga and make the energy rushing to you and you go nuts. I don't want you to do this type of thing.

Many people do a little bit of this practice, a little bit of that practice and sometimes a one year syllabus they make you do in one month. See if too much electricity goes what happen? The fuse blows. That sort of things happen or you get stomach problem or some other problem. So it is very important to grow gradually and steadily. That is why your body is getting prepared, practice Sri Sri Yoga and read some knowledge. We have such a composite programme in our yoga. It is so complete. There is Gyan Yoga, Bakti Yoga. Hollow and Empty meditation. If you are very good in meditation then it means that the Kundalini is already awaken. But when the people make you do all this forcibly and make Kundalini rise then it leads to complications. Then there are no beneficial results is what I have seen.

ONE OR DIFFERENT TYPES OF YOGA TECHNIQUES

Que: Is it Okey to mix Different Yoga techniques or should we find one way?

Gurudev: No, don't mix them, it becomes a hotch - potch You have on your platter such a wonderful programme. All based on a single line of thought, a philosophy which is ancient but profound and still modern. So just follow one way. That is the best.

I am saying this after many years. Otherwise I usually say, do whatever you like. Do you know why? I have got many people coming to me after going here and there and making a big mess of their mind. So now I have started putting my foot down and so I am telling you, don't do it.

Several people went here and there and were told to do this, Japa or that technique and later on they were uncontrollably shivering. These people have problems and had to go to hospital. Several such cases have happened over the past few years. People had to be given higher medication. And some of them have become so difficult to heal.

Why do you want to do other different techniques, what is the point? you have something very good on your platter. But if you are not at all getting benefitted, you tell me that this is not helping you at all.

Then I will show you where to go, which would help you.

NADI SHODAN PRANAYAMA

Que: Tell me something about ' Nadi shodan' alternate nostril pranayama

Gurudev: There are, 1,72,000 Nadis/energy channels in our body. When we breath these are activated and that is why we are alive. When we breathe through the left nostril, certain Nadis are functioning and others function when we breath through the right nostril. So when we alternative the breath through the nostrils, certain changes happen in the body and in our system.

Our system gets purified, fresh energy moves in the system and the stress is eliminated. The left nostril activates the functioning of the right brain and vice versa. So when we alternate our breathing all the brain waves get synchronised. Biochemical changes happen in the body. The endocrine glands function better and any imbalance in the body is rooted out. These are many benefits of pranayama.

MANTRAHS, YAGYAS, POOJA

Part III

MANTRAHS, YAGYAS, POOJA

GETTING RID OFF UNWANTED THOUGHTS

Que: Are you trying to get rid off unwanted thoughts? Try this simple technique to free your mind

Gurudev: When a thought arises in the mind it is not easy to get rid off it. The thought keeps coming back over and over again and if you decide to do something else, you will feel uneasy until finish with that thought; it becomes irritating like a grain of sand in the eye.

Similarly if you are unhappy about something that sadness does not easily leave you , what ever you do to get rid off it. Even by listening to inspiring discourses that sadness does not go away. Many times you tell your mind that something is trivial and not worry about it. But the mind or intellect does not pay any attention. So we can chant a Mantrah. Our mind learn the form of that mantrah we repeat.

'Mana Trayate iti Mantrah' means a Mantra is that which is brought to mind again and again. And to practice this mind and Mantrah should not be separate. The mind should become the Mantrah. If the mind thinks of something else while chanting the Mantrah, this Mantrah will not be effective. The mind should be filled with the Mantrah, The moment that happens the mind is free from worry.

A worry is something that is not in place. It neither is here nor there. A Mantrah is necessary to drive out worries. A Mantrah has strength and spirit. When these are present the mind becomes the power of the Mantrah. The power of mind and the power of Mantrah are the same.

'Chittam Mantrah' – Mind should become the Mantrah. The power of the every Mantrah can be felt in the form of vibrations. When an atom explodes its impacts spreads not only for many kilometers, but the effects remain for many years – all this from the explosion of one atom! The mind is thousand times subtler than an atom.

Mantrah is the cure for the mind, whether the mantrah is Om, 'Ram Ram' or 'Om Namasivaya' the effect of mantrah depends on the how it is pronounced and invoked.

You can control the mind by using a Mantrah. With help of Mantrah the mind loses its smallness and becomes vast, the mind that is dissatisfied becomes content and mind that is continuously disturbed by desires is released from them and find fulfillment.

Although a Mantrah may be the same its value is different when given by a Guru. Then you feel the power of the Mantrah. When your mind is at peace you can experience the real power of the Mantrah.

(Gurudev Sri. Sri.)

GAYATRI MANTRAH

Que: What is the significance of Gayatri Mantrah? Can women chant it? Why do we chant 108 times?

Gurudev: Om Bhur Bhuwah, Swah, Tat Savithur Varenyam Bhargo Devasya Deemahi Dhiyo yona Prachaodayat

Ga- Ya- Tri There are three types of misery. We have three bodies – the gross body, The subtle body and causal body. And all the three level there is misery. The human life has to cross over all the three and that is what Gayatri means- One who sings it, sails over the ocean of misery to go to bliss.

The Gayatri Mantrah is one of the greatest prayer mankind has. What does it say? Let me soak in the divine, destroy all my sins and let this divine light that burns all sins let me adore and soak in that Divine light and let the divinity inspire my intellect.

See, all our actions happen through our intellect, right? Thoughts come and you act. So you pray to the divine to bring good thought into your mind. you pray to the divine to take 'over my intellect inspire my intellect,' Dhiyo Yona Prachodayat.

Dhi means intellect, May my intellect be guided by, kindled by and inspired by you (Divinity).

When right thoughts come your actions will always be right. When intuitive thoughts come your actions will be fruitful. So praying for the best thought let my mind, my whole energy be socked in divinity. That is the significance of Gayatri Mantrah.

Why 108 times?

Because there are 9 planets and 12 constellations, when 9 planets revolve around 12 constellation it brings 108 kinds of changes. If there is anything wrong in these changes, it can be rectified with the positive energy of the Mantrahs.

Can women chant Gayatri Mantrah?

Yes- nowhere is it is said women cannot chant. It is unfortunate that some where in the middle ages these rights of the women were taken away. We have reinstated that in the Ashram. Many women are learning.

(Gurudev Sri. Sri.)

GURU POOJA
What is the significance of Guru Pooja?

Gurudev: Guru Pooja is the mother of all Mantrahs. The Maha Mantrah. You can make your whole body in such a way when it becomes invitation to the divine. Guru pooja is an ancient Sanskrit invocation, which invites the ascended and enlightened Masters to enter your space. The way the Mantrah is stated, there is no choice but for these divine energies to answer the call of Guru Pooja. As you give yourself to the process of your invocation, your energy aligns with the divine and as a result your vibration rises in wonderful ways. Practicing Guru Pooja on a regular basis will bring a different quality to your life. It awakens your inner divinity allowing you to access peaceful and blissful feelings throughout the day. It is a powerful tool used by many practitioners. And we would like offer to you opportunities to bring it into your daily life. A Sanskrit chant with 36 verses, Within this Mantrah there are 16 ways in which invoke the divinity through powerful ceremony and ritual.

It is way to make yourself being an offering to the divine while you receive the blessings that the Invocation brings. It is a way to consecrate sacred space in your environment, your home and around your sacred alter.

(Gurudev Sri. Sri.)

YAGYAS
What is the Significance of Yagyas

Gurudev: Discomfort happens on three levels – physical, mental and ethereal level. They are body mind and soul – Yagyas is that which takes you out of all three discomforts, brings you comfort on all three level, physical, mental and spiritual.

Yagya is that action which does not bind you, which does not limit you. it is an action which brings only good to you and others. It is yagna that purifies our life. purifies our mind purifies our actions.

When you honour the divine quality, do some good action, chant, sing don't think that you just do it for your own comfort, it is also creating ripples in the subtle atmosphere. The angels are happy every time you meditate and chant, sing with all love and joy. Then you are giving food for the angels. All those moments of devotion in your life have immensely enriched the subtle universe. it has brought abundance to that plane of existence nourished that plane of existence. In return you receive a lot of blessings from there.

Yagya has three aspects

1. Deva Pooja   2. Sangathi karana   3. Dana

Deva Pooja is honouring the divinity. honouring the subtle existence. Sangathi karana is bringing every one together, taking everyone along with you. It has another meaning. Among the different faculties of yours – body mind breath- bringing a harmony among them is also Sangathi karana.

Dana is giving, gifting. When you do charity you help someone who is really in need, then that soul on a physical level feels a sigh of relief and sigh of relief from that soul brings positive vibrations towards you.

These good deeds that you do bring you merit, which helps see you go deep inside. You should have certain merits in order to go into meditation also – not everybody can do it. When you do some charity and good work, then so many souls, so many people, feel happy. Then happiness come to you as blessing and that blessing helps you go deep in meditation.

(Gurudev Sri. Sri.)

OM
Significance of Om !

Om! is called the sound of one hand clapping. Om is the eternal sound. Om is the sound which is there in the Universe all the time.

All the saints in the past when they went deep in meditation, they just heard Om. So, Om means many things, It means love, eternity, purity, peace. Om is made up of several Dhatus, Ah, oo, ma. Just Ah has 19 meanings. You can derive some several 1000 meanings from Om. All these meaning are attributed to Om. Om is seed of the whole creation. Om is the sound of creation. In bible to it is said
'In the beginning there was a word and that word was with God and the word was God. That is Om!

There they don't say which word. The word is Om.

It is in all religion in one on other form. That is the true name' Ek Omkar Satnaam'. Om means truth, It is the name of the infinity or the Divinity. It means love. It is the origin of the Universe.

There is a beautiful verse in 'Guru Granth Sahib' which begins with 'Ek Omkar satnaam karta purakh' from Om everything has come, in Om every thing dwell and into Om every thing will dissolve - both matter and consciousness.

The best thing is that it is a complete vibration. 'Ah' affects the lower part the body. 'Oo' affect the middle part. 'Ma' affects the upper part. The total prana is represented by one syllable Om. Before birth we were part of that sound and after death we will merge with that sound, the sound of the spirit. So you can say many things about Om. There in a whole Upanishad, Mandukya Upanishad which is all about Om. Now why don't we take only Om as Mantra. We need any other Mantra to chant during meditation. Before meditation you chant Om and create the vibration, but for meditation you need different Mantras. Just Om is not used. Hari Om or Om Namasivaya or something else is used along with Om.

Only recluses, those who want to do nothing with the world or who are very old are allowed to do chant Om. Even then it is not advisable.

(Gurudev Sri. Sri.)

PART - 4

LESSONS FROM GAUTAM
BUDDHA AND THE MONK

LESSONS FROM GAUTAM BUDDHA AND THE MONK

BUDDHA AND LITTLE GIRL
Why did Buddha wait for the little girl?

Gurudev: Once upon a time Gautam Buddha visited a town. The entire town gathered and was waiting to listen to him. But he want on waiting. He kept looking backwards at the road expecting a little 13 year old girl to come. He happened to meet her on the road and she had told him 'wait for me I am going to give this food to my father at the farm. But I will be back in time. Don't forget, wait for me'.

Finally the elders of the town said to Gautam Buddha ' for whom are you waiting? Everybody important is present. You can start your discourse' Buddha replied ' But the person for whom I have come so far is not present yet. I have to wait'.

Finally the girl arrived and exclaimed ' I am a little late, but you kept your promise! I knew you would keep your promise because I have been waiting for since my first memory as child – when I first became aware. I think I was four years old when I first heard your name. Your name was enough to ring a bell in my heart. And since for ten long years I have been waiting.'

Buddha responded- 'you have not been waiting in vain – you are the person who has attracted me to this village.' At the end of this discourse that little girl was the only one who went to him and said 'Initiate me, I was waiting enough and now I want to be with you.' Buddha replied ' you have to be with me because your town is so far out. I cannot keep coming again and again, the road is long.' In that entire town not single person came up to him to be initiated into meditation other than that little girl.

At night as they are getting ready to sleep Buddha chief disciple Ananda asked Buddha. 'Master before you go to sleep I want ask you one question. Do you feel a certain pull towards certain space – just like a magnetic pull?' Buddha 'You are right Ananda that is how I decide my journey. When I feel someone thirsty is so thirsty, that without me there is no other way for them – I have to move in that direction.'

Master moves towards the disciple and the disciple moves towards the Master. Sooner or later they are bound to meet. The meeting is not of the body – the meeting is of the very soul. It is like when you bring two lamps close to each other, the lamps remain separate but their flames become one.

(Gurudev Sri. Sri.)

**BUDDHA NOT
FORGIVING THE PERSON**
**Why did Buddha the Epitome of Compassion not Forgive
the person?**

Gurudev: Buddha was in an assembly, a gentleman walked

furiously towards him. He thought Buddha was doing something wrong. He found his children meditating with Buddha for one or two hours every day. And he thought that if his children were engaged in business they could make money and be better of. So the father of the family was very upset and he said ' I am going to teach this man a lesson.' So he came and looked at Buddha with furiousness.

As soon as he came near Buddha all his other thoughts disappeared - But his anger was still there. He was shivering and he could not speak. No words would come out of his mouth. So he spat on Buddha's face. Buddha simply smiled. All other disciples around were gripped with anger. They were so angry but they could not react as Buddha was there. So everybody was holding their lips and fists tight. And this man could not stay longer. He spat and a few moments later he thought ' if I stay longer I will burst out.' So he ran away.

When Buddha did not react and say anything and just smiled the man could not sleep the whole night. It was the first time in his life, he met somebody who would just simile when he spat on his face.

He underwent such a transformation. Next day he came and fell at Buddha's feet and said in ' please pardon me.' I don't know what I did.'

Buddha said 'I cannot excuse you - now the disciples were shocked ! Buddha so compassionate, he always excused anybody, now he said he cannot ex cuse him? Not possible! Buddha had to explain because everybody was in a state of shock Buddha said well while You didn't do anything how can

I excuse you? What did you do. What wrong have you done?' The man replied the 'yesterday I spat on your face- I am the same person' Buddha replied 'that person is not here now.' If I ever meet that person on whom you spat, I will tell him to excuse you.' So, to me right now this person who is here you are wonderful. You have not done anything wrong.'

That is compassion, compassion is not making somebody culprit. And thereby saying okay I forgive you. That is not compassion. Your forgiveness should be such that the person who is being forgiven does not even know you are forgiving them. They should not even feel guilty for a minute. That is the right type of forgiveness. If you make someone feel guilty about their mistake then you have not forgiven them. That guilt itself is punishment. It is good enough.

(Gurudev Sri. Sri.)

COMING OUT OF THE CYCLE OF KARMA
How to come out of the cycle of karma

By not   reacting, and through wisdom and through meditation. All these take you out of Karma.

I will tell you a story. Lord Buddha had a devotee who was also his cousin. He was brilliant man and very devoted. In the beginning Buddha's Sangha or communion was quite small. But in time it became bigger. So the devotees close to Buddha became more possessive and his cousins felt that he owned Buddha. But Buddha can't be owned by any body. You cannot say you own an ocean. So because of this there were some misunderstandings and this cousin turned against Buddha. When some people have their own opinion or some negativity there are a few more people who will join them. This cousin of Buddha and few people became a group and one day when Buddha was giving a sermon, he went up to the hill pushed a boulder from there towards Buddha. The boulder stopped just few centimeters away from Buddha. Otherwise it would have killed him.

The other loyal disciples got so angry and upset. They said 'we have to punish him and teach him a lesson.' But Buddha stopped them and just smiled. he said 'it is karma, you don't do anything he will reap.

"Once in the 1990s I was in Washington D.C. I was giving a talk and there were 300 people there. Suddenly a tall hefty man came from the back to attack me. He said 'this is satan and devilish' everyone froze in their seats because nobody knew what to do. He could have lifted me in one hand as he was so big. I just looked into his eyes and said 'Wait'! it is not a time for me to go. I have come here to do some work. Let me complete my work' I didn't tell him that, I just said Wait! but in my mind I said I' am not ready to go!'. And then that guy looked at me and sat down in front of me and started crying. He came in 8 meters away and in anger and anguish but he just sat down and tears flowed from his eyes. To conclude the story short, he then joined our course and everything changed for him."

Why I am saying this is, every phenomenon that happens in and around us happens due to some karma. Having said that, It does not mean that is if something is fatalistic you simply accept that everything is karma and you can't do anything about it. No, that is wrong understanding of karma. Karma is phenomenon and you have the power change it, in the future because life is combination of free will and destiny. Your height is your destiny but your weight is your free will. If you weigh 100 kilograms you can't say well this is my fate. No, get into the thread mill and do some exercise. When a phenomenon happens and you react then the act keeps going on. Don't react but act.

When someone pushed the boulder at Buddha what the people did was they reacted. But Buddha asked them not to react and he smiled. That is an action. When someone is against you if you show love and compassion and if you turned the other cheek when they hit you they cannot hit you back. That is bigger weapon. The principle of nonviolence is also an action a more intelligent and wise action and not just a reaction.

(Gurudev Sri. Sri.)

MONK STEALING
What made this Monk Steal from the palace

There was a great monk who lived in the Himalayas. He had free access anywhere he went, because people loved and welcomed him. This monk is to go to the king's palace and have his lunch there every day. The queen would serve him lunch in a golden plate and a cup. He would go eat and walk out. This was his routine. One day after his meal he grabbed a silver glass and golden spoon and took it with him. He didn't even tell that he was taking it , that he wanted it or anything.

People in the palace noticed. He would never take anything. What happened today? He took these things with him without telling anybody. He just put in his bag and left.

Three days later he brought back the cup and spoon and left it there. This was even more puzzling. Before they thought may be needed it, so he took it. Now he came and put it back it was more puzzling.

So the King called all wise people and enquired as to why this happened. Why did he take it and then bring it back. They found all the wise people and pundits who said 'find out what you fed him the previous day or two.'

So they went and found out all that information. They found they had fed him food they confiscated from some robbers (some decoits). They had found and arrested a few decoits a couple of days ago and they confiscated a lot of grain and food stuffs (everything from them). That was then cooked and served to the saint and made him rob the things from the palace. In ancient days people used to look into all these things. If somebody did something very unusual they went into the root cause of it why?. Instead of accusing the monk who started stealing... what made the monk steal? The food! who cooked the food, what was done in the food and what happened ? They went into the details and found the root cause of it.

It is ignorance to think that we are the doers. And the way to come out of this ignorance is definite understanding definite knowledge in the mind that my body and the world is undergoing changes all the time. The entire Universe is in the form of fluids, It is in the state of fluidity, and it is all full of change, going on its own , according to the nature.

The definite knowledge 'I am not the body I am the self, I am the space, I am the imperishable, untouched, untained by the prakrity (nature) by the world around me. This body is hollow and empty. And every particle in this body is changing. This mind is changing and changing. This definite knowledge is the way out of the cycle.

(Gurudev Sri. Sri.)

ENLIGHTENMENT, KNOWLEDGE AND KARMA

ENLIGHTENMENT, KNOWLEDGE AND KARMA

Seven Questions About Enlightenment -

a.   How long should I meditate to get enlightenment?

Gurudev: There is no limit. Time will do it. Your job is to keep the window open, but time will bring the sun light. You can't make Sun light come into your house just because you have opened the window. You can't say "I opened the window but the sun light has not come yet". If you keep your shutters on even with the sun has risen you will remain in darkness. So your effort is needed.

b.   Can married couple also get enlightenment?

Gurudev: See, the example of Ramakrishna Paramhamsaji, He was married. Sharada Devi was his wife. There are many such examples like this. So even couples can attain enlightenment. Enlightenment is not something that just drop from somewhere. It is present in all of us.

c.   If the purpose of life is to attain liberation is there any value of all the time we spend in our education, profession and career?

Gurudev: Each one has own place. You need to do both. To make both you need to work and to grow the spiritual path. You need to meditate Both go together. They do not oppose each other.

d   Often we think that only when we leave everything will be able to meditate.
That is not the case. We see many people who have left everything and sit here but they take up something else to occupy their mind

Gurudev: It is not necessary that you have to leave everything and then meditate. If you have taken up some responsibility fulfill it.

e   The word enlightenment is used so many times that is why it is so confusing. Enlightenment is simply peeling off layers and becoming hollow and empty. Get to the spot where you feel absolutely comfort and absolute freedom.

f   That is liberating, that is Nirvana, that is self realisation, that is yoga and that is unity.

g   You can call it by so many names. And too much reading also lead to confusion that is why I say be natural, be simple.

FOUR PILLARS OF KNOWLEDGE

Q. Gurudev What are the pillars of knowledge? How can

they be useful for both inner and outer growth? Please explain the secrete behind them?

Gurudev: To reach the self, there are four major tools, the four Pillars of Knowledge: The first one is called Viveka.

Viveka is grossly translated as discrimination, but it's not just discrimination. Viveka is the understanding or observation that everything is changing. What ever you consider as stationary or solid is neither stationary nor solid. Everything is changing. Existence is an ever changing reality."Our own bodies are changing. Every minute new cells are born and old cells are dying. Every time you breathe, old energy goes out and new energy comes in. Our body is a bundle of atoms and atoms are always disintegrating. Our thoughts and emotions are changing. You are not the same person you were yesterday. You cannot maintain the same degree of happiness or sadness all the time. It fluctuates. Emotions, feelings, view points are all changing.""But there is something different from all this that is not changing. The one who is observing the change is non-changing, otherwise how can one recognize the change? The reference point to recognize change has to be non-changing. Discriminating between that which is not changing, and everything else which is ever changing is "Viveka". Understanding that everything in this world is changing would reduce 99% of the misery in this world.

The second pillar is called Vairagya. Vairagya is translated as Dispassion. Behind every misery there is hope. Hope is the fuel for miserable people. There is deep desire for some joy in the future: If I change my town, I will be happy. If I change my relationship, or my job, or my company, I will be happier. People who are single think they will be happy if they get married. Married people think they were better off when they were single. A child thinks when he/she grows up and goes to college they will happy. A college student says "Once I get a job I will be happy". A manager says "When I become the director I will be happy" Postponing happiness sometime in the future can make you miserable right now. "Pleasure can also tire you. How long can you look at something beautiful? Eventually you will get tired of it; your eyelids will fall off. How long can you smell a beautiful fragrance? People working in the perfume factories are sick of perfumes. If you like donuts, how many can you stuff through your mouth? How much ice-cream can you enjoy? Music- how much can you hear? Touching, and being touched, how long can you enjoy? The world is full of pleasure for the five senses, but the senses have their limitations. But the mind wants endless joy. An attitude of "So what! Let it be, whatever" takes away the fevourishness in you and brings you to that pillar of dispassion. "Dispassion" is NOT apathy! Often we think dispassion means being unenthusiastic, depressed and not interested in anything. This is not dispassion! Dispassion is lack of fevourishness. Dispassion is full of activity and enthusiasm, yet devoid of fevourishness. Dispassion towards the enjoyments of the five sense or the spiritual enjoyment, towards the seen and the unseen, the outer world or the inner world, is the second pillar of knowledge.

The third pillar consists of the Six Wealths. The Vedas have mentioned six types of Wealths: Shama, Dama, Uparati, Titiksha, Shraddha, and Samadhana.

The first wealth is Shama. Shama is tranquility of the mind. When the mind wants to do too many things, it gets completely scattered. When shama is established, you are able to focus and your mind is more alert. When dispassion is firmly established, shama automatically starts happening, the mind is tranquil.

The second wealth is Dama. Dama means control over senses, the ability to have a say over one's senses. Many times you don't want to say something, yet you do. Many times you don't want to look at something, yet you look anyway. You decided you are full and you will not eat anymore. Then some nice food is served, and it smells so good that you go ahead and take a bite, and another. Soon, to your surprise, you find that you have stuffed in more than your tummy can take. Having Dama, you are not carried away by our senses. You will say "Yes" or "No" to the senses, not the other way around.

The third wealth is Titiksha. Titiksha means endurance or forbearing. When difficult things come, forbearance allows you to go on without getting completely shaken. In life, some pleasant events happen, some unpleasant events happen. So what! None of them stay forever. Health comes and sickness comes. Moods come and go. Profits come and losses come. People come and go in life. Titiksha is not getting shaken by what happens. Often what is unpleasant can become pleasant later on. What you thought was very bad, later on was found to be very good for you. It made you strong. Understanding this helps not hanging on to the past and not judging events as good or bad. The ability to not to get carried away by the events is Titiksha. When you play a game, winning and loosing is a part of it. The game has more value when it is a little tough. If you already knew who will win the game, you will loose interest in the game. Look at life as a game. Just turn back and look at all the difficult situations you have gone through in life. In spite of it all, you are complete today. The difficulties could not destroy you. They only made you stronger. You are more powerful than them.

The fourth wealth is Uparati. Uparati means rejoicing in your own nature, being with your nature. Often you are not with your nature, you or doing things because someone else says or does something. Often people do things for approval from others. Being in the present moment, being the joy that you are, the ability to rejoice in anything that you do, that is Uparati. Letting go of everything, being playful is Uparati, and then taking everything seriously is also Uparati. These are completely opposite values, but taking them together, living them together, that is Uparati.

The fifth wealth is Shraddha. Shraddha means faith. Faith is needed when you have found the limit of your knowledge. You know something this far, and you don't know anything beyond that. Your willingness to know the unknown is Shraddha, the faith. If your mind is fixed, and says "That's it. I know it all", that is ego. The more you know, the more will be the feeling that you don't know. Recognition of the unknown is Shraddha. Faith in your self, faith in the Master, faith in the Divine, faith in the infinite order of things, faith in that love of infinity, is Shraddha. Observe the nature of doubt. Doubt is always about something positive. When someone says, "I love you", you doubt asking "Really"? But when someone says, "I hate you, I am angry at you", then you don't doubt it, you don't ask "Really?". Doubt the negative, and be confident of the positive. Without faith, it would be like someone saying, "First let me learn how to swim, then I will get into the water". You have to get into the water to learn swimming. The entire world works on faith. For example, any system, whether a credit card system, airlines, banks, even a medical system, although there is no guarantee, there is a high probability that everything will work the way it is meant to. If there could be 100 percent probability, then there would be no need of faith. When there is less than 100 percent probability, that means the result is not knowledge, it is based on faith.

The sixth wealth is Samadhan. Samadhan means being at ease, being content. How do you feel when you are at ease? How does it feel when you are totally at ease, calm and serene? Being at ease with you, at ease with the people and situations around you, with the whole existence, is Samadhan. This is a great wealth by itself. These six wealths together form the third pillar.

The fourth pillar is called Mumukshatva. Mumukshatva is the desire for the highest, a desire for total freedom, for enlightenment, whatever you want to call it. First of all you can desire something only when you feel it is possible for you. When you think it is not possible, then you cannot even desire it. When you think enlightenment is not possible for you, then slowly you eliminate the possibility, and then the next possibility, and then the next. Mumukshatva is present when there is a deep desire for the highest, a burning desire, a longing for the Divine.""When there is a desire in someone to learn, it should come from within. Don't think you have to attain it. Think you already have it. To some degree, to some extent, you have all the six wealths also. If you put a little more attention on them, they become stronger and more solid in you. The pillars are already there, you only have to make them stronger, build them a little higher.

TYPES OF MISERY
Three Types Of Misery

The Indian philosophy caters three types of misery. (1) physical (2) mental (3) spiritual. Spiritual torment is the worst. The agony and the torment that one experiences is at the level of the mind and go beyond the thoughts is purpose of samadhi. Mind is the cause of both bondage and liberation. Unless one knows how to quiten the mind it is impossible to achieve the inner peace.

The mind can be transcended through Yoga Sadhana. Yoga is not asanas alone. Pranayama and meditation are integral part of it. Pathanjali Yoga Darshan, Adi Sankara's Dig Drishya, Viveka, Shainism, Thirumandrum of Saint Thirumala all offer different techniques that help one to overcome spiritual torment and misery.

Ayundreda, Yoga and Vedanta respectively are the three remedies to eliminate mala (impurities in the body) Vikshepa (disturbances in the mind) and Avarana (Veil the covers that light on the air). While Ayundreda, help people to calm their thought, pranayama and meditation help one become happy from the core of their being.

Happiness is only a sign of connection with the divinity deep within. Through these Vedantic practices you can experience the scintillating consciousness that you are. It is a simple recognition of what is around has always been in one and within as our self.

The basic principle of Vedanta is that what you are seeing is already there, like air around you. You don't have to go somewhere searching. You only need to become aware in the same way as divinity or your consciousness, bliss, love is already present in you. It is only a matter of recognizing it.

Scientific temper and Vedantic knowledge together make the whole and bring inner stillness. And that is the essence of Indian spirituality. What is spirituality if under privileged are not taken care of. What they fail to see is that where ever there is genuine spirituality a component of Seva or service has always been attached to it.

In the realm of consciousness, as you sow you shall reap. If you think suffering is an important tool for uniting with God then you are bound to attract it. If you sow a seed of suffering that multiplies, thus lack of experience of Dhyana (meditation) and Samadhi (Equanimity) can keep a seeker morose and dull. To overcome this one need shift in understanding about heaven and hell and about consciousness that is all pervading. Spirituality alone can bring that shift.

In the Eastern philosophy experience come first and then faith follows. In the occidental way of thinking belief come first and then experience. It was experience which turned atheist Vivekanda into a Swami.

UNDERSTANDING KNOWLEDGE

Que: Sometimes I am not able to understand the knowledge given by you. What should I do so that I can get both your love an knowledge?

Gurudev: What ever you find difficult to understand it is not to be understood at all. If it all going above your head, let it go. Take only what you can understand. See every ones capacity to gain knowledge is different. But to be in love, to be in devotion you don't need any capabilities. When it comes to devotion every one is same and equally capable. There is no special qualification for it.

Now, when we talk about knowledge seems yes, everyone has a different capacity. Some people have a higher capacity for knowledge and some lesser capacity, but this does not make any difference when there is devotion and a feeling of oneness.

Don't think that if you are knowledgeable God become happy with you or become fond of you. It is not that. The purpose of knowledge is for your own joy. To purify you intellect you need knowledge. To purify your heart you need love. To purify your karma you need seva. All these should go together.

DEEP REST

Just say one thing to your self. I want nothing. This wanting nothing gives you the deepest of the rests.

Rest is not just physically lying on the bed, it is mood of the mind which says ' I am satisfied' I am content.' It is only contentment which can give you rest. And this contentment is not going to come to you by doing some things or by engaging in any activity. It will come to you only through knowledge and knowledge and knowledge.

1.   Every thing is impermanent.

2.   I am satisfied.

3.   I want nothing

This is the essence of knowledge.

(Gurudev Sri. Sri.)

INGREDIENTS TO BE SUCCESSFUL

Que: What are the ingredients to be successful? How come Lord Krishna found success in everything he did.?

Gurudev: For success in life you need Yukti (skill) and Shakti (strength), Bakti (devotion) and Mukti, (Freedom and love in personal life)

Without freedom you will find no love. And without love there is no joy. Freedom doesn't mean doing anything. You follow some norms, a little discipline. And in social life you need Sakti and Yukt; strength and skill. And this is what Ramayana and Mahabharata tell you. Though Duryodhana had all the power but he had no Yukti no bakti. The skill was with Krishna and so he won. In life you need yukti (skill) and shakti (strength) bakti (devotion) and Mukti (freedom and love in personal life).

KARMAS OF THE PAST

Que: Gurudev I am very troubled thinking about all the Karmas of my past life.

Please advice and guide me.

Gurudev: Just know that the seeds of all such karmas of the past lives get burnt once you come here. So just relax and be happy.

Suppose you have a house that has been locked away for a hundred years. Now you will ask " Oh Gurudev how can I remove the darkness of hundred years in just a day?

I tell you the moment the lamp of knowledege has been lit in your heart all the darkness (of ignorance and negativity) vanishes away in an instant. Karmas burn away as you go deeper and deeper into self knowledge.
when you realise with the awareness that I am not the body, I am the eternal spirit, any negative effects of your past karmas will simply disappear without affecting you.

MISCELLANEOUS

MISCELLANEOUS

FACTORS AFFECTING THE LIFE OF AN INFANT

There are four factors that affect the life of an infant. 25% is attributed to the impressions that they carry from their past life time. The next 25% of impression comes from the mother and father. 25% of the impressions are caught on from the immediate environment that they are in. The kind of environment and the company they keep play a big role in this. The remaining 25% of the impressions come from the kind of actions a person does by himself. So in this way many things make an impression in the life of an infant. A teacher makes a big impression in the life of a person.

(Gurudev Sri. Sri.)

POLITICS IN THE PATH

Que: Gurudev, I want to become a teacher and spread this wonderful knowledge but I am disturbed sometimes by the politics that seen in this path, kindly guide me.

Gurudev: Where ever there are people there will be Politics. Politics means everybody has their own tendencies and human being have tendencies. In this world, in any field, or any path any where you go and none find everybody to be alike. If in your mind you think everybody should behave in the same way or have the same attitude same mentality or same level of growth then you are making a big mistake.

The spiritual path is like going to school. All children in a school cannot be in the same class. Some are in A grade, some in B grade and some are in C. some are in 8th Standard some in 9th. Even in a school, there are kids of all age groups and all ranges of intelligence. Any path is like that. And the spiritual path is a place where some have just stepped in. Some have been there for sometime. There are some cases who fail in a class for many years, you can't just look at them and say you don't want to go to that class. You have to go to that class ! Sometimes someone get stuck in one place.

Sometimes people ask me why do I keep some very tough and rough people here and there (in the Art of Living). I say that I keep them close so that the world is free from them sometime. Some people who are too troublesome their parents say Gurudev we cannot handle him at home, so you please take care of him.' And can I say no? So I say Okay.

I give a long long rope and enough room for people to transform. You don't worry about them, It is my karma (duty). I cater all types of people. I have said. 'Accept people as they are'. So I cannot go back in my words! I am stuck.

In every field there are people who are exception to the rule, or black sheep in that field. You shouldn't look at one as someone else and make a concept in your mind or be prejudiced towards them. This is very important. Prejudice kills people.

WORSHIPPING ANCESTORS
Why do we Worship our Ancestors?

Gurudev: The subtle Brahman is only one, Yet it is not one. The subtle consciousness has many layers to it. The spirit is one, yet it is many. The whole universe is permeated by the spirit, by Brahman yet to different degrees.

For example stones have life and gender. As anthropologist and biologist know that plants and trees can be male and female. So this can be for stones. The ancient people of every culture knew this. The Shilpis (stone masons) in India knew to identify which stone is male and which is female. The native American chose certain stones for their worships and prayer.

Stones have one unit of life

Water has got two units of life

Fire has three units of life Space has five units of life Trees have 6 units of life Animals have 7 units of life
Human beings have 8 units of life. And are known as Astavasu.
Super human blossomed being who do extraordinary work, whether it be very good or very bad have 9 units of life.

Further more human can develop up to 16 units of life. When we die we become more powerful in some way. We go between 9 and 10 units of life. This is strange but true. That is why ancestors are worshiped. The moment this body drops, the spirit has become free without boundaries and nothing can stop it, the spirit moves around freely. If it is bound in the body you have only 8 units of life you only reach out to some. When you have 9 units you have a little more power but if you die then you have access to the 9th and 10th units, so you gain much more access to the planets. That is why ancestors have capacity to bless you because their spirit freed from the limited body, can know cognize, can bless you. You can feel their presence. So when you pray to them they can grant you certain boons. They are able to bestow unto you to what ever extent they are powerful. Ancestral worship can be found from China to Latin American countries.

In the Christian tradition there is All Souls Day, where you respect the souls and ask for their blessings. This is one of reasons why bodies are buried behind the church to make the place more powerful. Ancestors have got one more unit of power and are called as Pitras.

(Gurudev Sri. Sri.)

AWAKENING OF DIVINITY
Focus and expansion

Focus sharpens the mind and relaxation expands the mind. Just an expanded mind without sharpness cannot bring the holistic development. At the same time, just the sharp mind without expansion causes tension, angry and frustration. The balance between the focussed mind and expanded consciousness bring perfection. Both Sudarshan Kriya and Advanced course techniques are aimed at developing such consciousness, with sharp and unbounded. Seva and commitment play a major role in this. Also food and attitude have an effect. Expanded consciousness is peace and joy. Focused consciousness is love and creativity. A point of focused consciousness is individual self. When every atom of the expanded consciousness becomes sharp, focused, that is the Awakening of Divinity.

(Gurudev Sri. Sri.)

REPEATING BASIC COURSE

Que: Guruji is it important to repeat the Basic course / Happiness programme?

Gurudev: During any of our course what is visible is not the motive. On a subtle level within your consciousness there is change related to those process those stories those knowledge points and that the reason you feel a change within yourself after the course. Just like in one of the process, sharing your life story is not the objective, but what happening actively is that you feel some lightness within you, you get rid of deep life impression that bother you. Similarly there is something important related to each and every process, story and even your home work. The more you give into each the more get out of it. Now what many of you think – why go again and repeat all that been have gone through? We know that what is being taught during course: we have already learned Sudarshan Kriya and continue with our daily practice. Then what is point in repeating all such concepts. I tell you every time you repeat the course you will find it absolutely new, always! How many of the repeaters have this experience? It is not just you but other participants as well because of whom you complete the course. And every time there is lot of new participants which means it is all new level of Happiness.

Your experience in Sudarshan Kriya get more deep every time you repeat the course because very time you come you learn about small mistakes that you make. Ujjai breath still is challenge for many and there are people who are not able to follow the Kriya Rhythm, especially the faster circles. They are on their own breathing as far as possible – no! follow the Manthra 'Sohum precisely. It is important your practice gets more towards perfection when you are corrected for your mistakes.

Similarly many of you don't even remember how many layers are we all living on. Knowing and remembering about yourself is the most important aspect of our life, else what is the difference between you and robot?

Golden keys shared with you during course are most precious as they are the crux of your life - applicable to any situation, at the same time they need repetitive hammering because once your have done with the course over time, you start getting stained back in your normal life.

I suggest you all, including the teachers keep repeating the Basic/ Happiness programme at least once in six months.

Get all the doubts out of your mind and just come and sit. I will be there to welcome you. Have this faith.

ASTROLOGY

Que: Gurudev my parents deeply follow astrology and force me into it. Should I follow it or Shudarshan Kriya sufficient to get rid off negativity?

Gurudev: Yes this is good enough. Astrology is a science, our ancient gift to the world, but too much into it also ignorance, and discarding it totally also ignorance. Knowledge of astrology is good, but 'Om Namasivaya' is the best remedy to all astrological problems.

EFFECTIVE COMMUNICATION
The Six secretes of Effective Communication

We start communication from the instant we take our first breath. Our first cry is a communication to our mother, and to the world - that we have arrived. And till our last breath we are in constant communication.

Yet good communication is much more than mere words. It is an art and effective communication has dimensions that are larger than what is spoken. The ability to communicate affectionately with one and all is a skill worth possessing.

Be sensitive and Sensible

Communication is a dialogue, not a monologue.
We must respect the view point of the person or persons we are communicating with.

Communication is the act of being sensitive and sensible at the same time. Some people were too sensitive and losing their sensibleness. Their speech lacks clarity and is inarticulate. And there are people who make perfect sense, but they are insensitive. They say correct things, but they are not aware the emotional responses of the other. We need that beautiful combination of sensitivity and sensibleness.

Your state of mind matters

You cannot improve someone by getting angry at them. You only ruin your peace of mind.

When you are angry nobody wants to hear it. Even though you are saying the correct thing, your communication does not have the impact it ought to have had. Your mental state is heard by your listeners before the words. A calm state of mind and a smile will conquer the most defiant, difficult of people.

Humour coupled with care and concern

A good sense of humour relieves you from fear and anxiety. Humour is not just about words, reading and repeating jokes. It is the lightness of your being, that bring out the authentic habit. And this lightness comes up with taking life itself not too seriously. Having a sense belongingness with everybody including those who are not practicing yoga and meditation having unstable faith in the Divine being in the company of those who live in knowledge and humours.

Heart To Heart Communication

Almost all the relation ship breakdown due to too much talking and explain about oneself. ' I am this way, don't mistake me, don't misunderstand me'. If you keep silence when required everything will work out much better. Don't explain things of the past, brood over them, or ask for explanations. When the heart speaks and heart listens - harmony is produced.

Real communication is beyond words

All of us have experienced one time or the other, an amazing phenomenon whether in one to one communication or in addressing a huge audience. Something intangible moves people more than the words. We try to rationalize by attribute this to charm, charisma, presence, body language etc.

If you are firmly established in this zone of silence, if your mind is calm you will find yourself suddenly being able to influence individuals, groups and masses.

Be a good listener

The single most important skill in the art of good communication is the skill of listening. Listening not just to wards, but also to feelings and expressions. Observe infants. They listen to expressions and gestures. Even without understanding words they communicate with you. Some where in the journey of life we have lost this ability. Let's make an attempt to regain it.

This world is varied, beyond our imagination. We need to establish communication on three level, communication with oneself, communication with society and communication with nature. There is always something to share learn and teach.

TEMPLE VISITING

Que:The more I gain knowledge from Sadhana, Seva, Satsang my faith in worshiping idol and visiting physical temple is going down. What is that Guruji?

Gurudev: Yes, it is okey that you don't go to temples after temples. Where ever you are, meditate and you find the divinity. The divine is everywhere. you don't have to run to temples. This is the first stage, You have crossed that stage and have come to the second stage where Hari comes to you. There is a saying that when Kabeer was calling Hari.. Hari.. Hari. He did'nt find Hari. But when he started meditating he said, Hari is coming to me where ever I am.

RESISTING CHANGES
Que: Why do people resist change?

Gurudev: People resist change because they are afraid that they would lose something precious, all changes could bring out a disaster for them. But if you communicate to them that change would make them better they would definitely take it. Nobody dislikes climbing up the ladder. People do want something positive, more happiness or whatever. What we need to do it is to communicate better with them speak in their language, and explain that the change will make things better. It will take some time, it cannot happen overnight it takes some persuasion but it does happen.

MARRIAGE

Marriage is to give and take or compromise. You cannot say 'I want it this way only.' No, you have to let go your wish and desires and listen what other person wants. You have to compromise somewhere in between. If there is no compromise then there are arguments, when there are arguments then the fight happens.

(Gurudev Sri. Sri.)

www.ingramcontent.com/pod-product-compliance
Lightning Source LLC
LaVergne TN
LVHW020609200726
843509LV00001B/40